CICERO

De Amicitia
Selections
Teacher's Guide

Patsy Rodden Ricks & Sheila K. Dickison

Bolchazy-Carducci Publishers, Inc.
Wauconda, Illinois USA

Editor
LeaAnn A. Osburn

Cover Design
Adam Phillip Velez

Cicero
De Amicitia Selections
Teacher's Guide

Patsy Rodden Ricks & Sheila K. Dickison

© 2006 Bolchazy-Carducci Publishers, Inc.
All rights reserved.

Bolchazy-Carducci Publishers, Inc.
1000 Brown Street
Wauconda, IL 60084 USA
www.bolchazy.com

Printed in the United States of America
2006
by United Graphics

ISBN-13: 978-0-86516-641-7
ISBN-10: 0-86516-641-2

Contents

Preface

The authors have written the Teacher's Guide to *Cicero: De Amicitia Selections* to provide useful resources for the classroom. While this book follows the Advanced Placement selections of the *De Amicitia*, we hope that all teachers will find this book a pleasant and useful guide to Cicero.

The book is divided into six sections.

LARGE SIZE TEXT

An enlarged copy of the Latin text is included and may be reproduced on transparencies for an overhead projector.

A PowerPoint slide show of the Latin text of *de Amicitia* is also available to teachers and is extremely effective for the classroom, largely due to the pen option that makes it easy for the teacher to point out constructions and words.

A link to the PowerPoint presentation is available for downloading at http://www.bolchazy.com/ below the description of *De Amicitia*. After clicking on the link, the prompt will ask if the file should be opened or saved. Select "save" and choose the location on your computer where you would like the file to be saved. If you prefer, the direct link is http://www.bolchazy.com/prod.php?cat=new&id=6390.

Either Microsoft Office PowerPoint or PowerPoint Viewer must be installed on your computer to use the slide show. If you do not have the PowerPoint Viewer, it is available at http://www.microsoft.com/downloads/details.aspx?FamilyID=428d5727-43ab-4f24-90b7-a94784af71a4&displaylang=en or go to http://www.microsoft.com/downloads and locate the PowerPoint Viewer 2003 download. The Windows version is called ppviewer.exe and the Mac version is called PPT98VW.HQX.

Once the PowerPoint or PowerPoint Viewer is installed on your computer, double click on the saved file: "cicero.ppt" and the slide show will open.

LITERAL TRANSLATIONS

The purpose of the translations is to match the Latin in construction, voice, and tense. It is not meant to be graceful and literary.

POINTS TO PONDER WITH ANSWERS

The "Points to Ponder" from the student text are reproduced here along with answers that do **not** strive to be inclusive or absolute but are only intended to be an introductory appraisal of the topic. A careful consideration of the Latin text will offer fuller answers to the teacher and students.

SAMPLE ASSESSMENTS

The three assessments included in this teacher's guide may be reproduced. They follow the form of Advanced Placement testing and include a spot question, a translation passage, and a short discussion question. In addition, optional questions that ask the student to define vocabulary in context and identify grammatical constructions have been included for teachers who wish to test these aspects of the student's knowledge.

DISCUSSION QUESTIONS

Questions about the passages have been written to stimulate the students to think about the larger implications of the text. They should serve as a complement to the "Points to Ponder" found in the textbook.

ANNOTATED BIBLIOGRAPHY

The annotated bibliography contains additional information about the sources listed in the bibliography of the student text.

Patsy Rodden Ricks
Sheila K. Dickison

LARGE SIZE TEXT

SELECTION A: LINES 1–107 [SECTIONS V.17–VI.23]

PART 1: LINES 1–28

[V. 17] *Laelius.* Ego vos hortari tantum possum ut amicitiam omnibus rebus humanis anteponatis; nihil est enim tam naturae aptum, tam conveniens ad res vel secundas vel adversas.

5 **[18]** Sed hoc primum sentio nisi in bonis amicitiam esse non posse; neque id ad vivum reseco, ut illi qui haec subtilius disserunt, fortasse vere, sed ad communem utilitatem parum; negant enim quemquam virum bonum esse nisi sapientem.

10 Sit ita sane; sed eam sapientiam interpretantur quam adhuc mortalis nemo est consecutus. Nos autem ea quae sunt in usu vitaque communi, non ea quae finguntur aut optantur, spectare debemus. Nunquam ego dicam C. Fabricium, M'. Curium, Ti.

15 Coruncanium, quos sapientes nostri maiores iudicabant, ad istorum normam fuisse sapientes. Qua

re sibi habeant sapientiae nomen et invidiosum et obscurum; concedant ut hi boni viri fuerint. Ne id quidem facient; negabunt id nisi sapienti posse

20 concedi. **[19]** Agamus igitur pingui Minerva, ut aiunt. Qui ita se gerunt, ita vivunt, ut eorum probetur fides, integritas, aequitas, liberalitas, nec sit in eis ulla cupiditas, libido, audacia, sintque magna constantia, ut ei fuerunt modo quos

25 nominavi, hos viros bonos, ut habiti sunt, sic etiam appellandos putemus, quia sequantur quantum homines possunt naturam optimam bene vivendi ducem.

PART 2: LINES 29–43

Sic enim mihi perspicere videor, ita natos esse

30 nos ut inter omnes esset societas quaedam, maior autem, ut quisque proxime accederet. Itaque cives potiores quam peregrini, propinqui quam alieni: cum his enim amicitiam natura ipsa peperit, sed ea non satis habet firmitatis. Namque hoc praestat

35   amicitia propinquitati quod ex propinquitate benevolentia tolli potest, ex amicitia non potest: sublata enim benevolentia amicitiae nomen tollitur,
propinquitatis manet. **[20]** Quanta autem vis
amicitiae sit ex hoc intellegi maxime potest, quod
40   ex infinita societate generis humani, quam conciliavit ipsa natura, ita contracta res est et adducta in
angustum ut omnis caritas aut inter duos aut inter
paucos iungeretur.

PART 3: LINES 44–65

[VI.] Est autem amicitia nihil aliud nisi omnium
45   divinarum humanarumque rerum cum benevolentia et caritate consensio; qua quidem haud scio
an excepta sapientia nil unquam melius homini
sit a dis immortalibus datum. Divitias alii praeponunt, bonam alii valetudinem, alii potentiam,
50   alii honores, multi etiam voluptates. Beluarum hoc
quidem extremum; illa autem superiora caduca et
incerta, posita non tam in consiliis nostris quam
in fortunae temeritate. Qui autem in virtute summum bonum ponunt, praeclare illi quidem, sed

55   haec ipsa virtus amicitiam et gignit et continet,
      nec sine virtute amicitia esse ullo pacto potest.
      [21] Iam virtutem ex consuetudine vitae ser-
      monisque nostri interpretemur, nec eam, ut
      quidam docti, verborum magnificentia metiamur,
60   virosque bonos eos qui habentur numeremus,
      Paulos, Catones, Gallos, Scipiones, Philos: his com-
      munis vita contenta est: eos autem omittamus qui
      omnino nusquam reperiuntur. Tales igitur inter
      viros amicitia tantas opportunitates habet quantas
65   vix queo dicere.

PART 4: LINES 66–87

[22] Principio, qui potest esse vita vitalis, ut ait
Ennius, quae non in amici mutua benevolentia
conquiescat? Quid dulcius quam habere quicum
omnia audeas sic loqui ut tecum? Qui esset tantus
70   fructus in prosperis rebus, nisi haberes qui illis
aeque ac tu ipse gauderet? Adversas vero ferre difficile esset sine eo qui illas gravius etiam quam
tu ferret. Denique ceterae res quae expetuntur
opportunae sunt singulae rebus fere singulis;

75   divitiae ut utare; opes ut colare; honores ut laudere; voluptates ut gaudeas; valetudo ut dolore careas et muneribus fungare corporis: amicitia res plurimas continet. Quoquo te verteris praesto est: nullo loco excluditur: nunquam intempestiva,

80   nunquam molesta est. Itaque non aqua, non igni, ut aiunt, locis pluribus utimur quam amicitia. Neque ego nunc de vulgari aut de mediocri, quae tamen ipsa et delectat et prodest, sed de vera et perfecta loquor, qualis eorum qui pauci nominantur

85   fuit. Nam et secundas res splendidiores facit amicitia, et adversas partiens communicansque leviores.

Part 5: Lines 88–107

[VII. 23] Cumque plurimas et maximas commoditates amicitia contineat, tum illa nimirum

90   praestat omnibus, quod bonam spem praelucet in posterum nec debilitari animos aut cadere patitur. Verum enim amicum qui intuetur, tamquam exemplar aliquod intuetur sui. Quocirca et absentes adsunt et egentes abundant et imbecilli

95 valent, et, quod difficilius dictu est, mortui vivunt; tantus eos honos, memoria, desiderium prosequitur amicorum, ex quo illorum beata mors videtur, horum vita laudabilis. Quod si exemeris ex rerum natura benevolentiae coniunctionem, nec

100 domus ulla nec urbs stare poterit; ne agri quidem cultus permanebit. Id si minus intellegitur, quanta vis amicitiae concordiaeque sit ex dissensionibus atque discordiis percipi potest. Quae enim domus tam stabilis, quae tam firma civitas est,

105 quae non odiis atque discidiis funditus possit everti? ex quo quantum boni sit in amicitia iudicari potest.

SELECTION B: LINES 1–63 [SECTIONS XXVII.100B–104]

PART 6: LINES 1–37

[100] [XXVII.] Virtus, virtus, inquam, C. Fanni et
tu, Q. Muci, et conciliat amicitias et conservat. In
ea est enim convenientia rerum, in ea stabilitas, in
ea constantia, quae cum se extulit et ostendit lumen
5   suum et idem adspexit agnovitque in alio, ad id se
admovet vicissimque accipit illud quod in altero est,
ex quo exardescit sive amor sive amicitia. Utrumque
enim dictum est ab amando; amare autem nihil aliud est nisi eum ipsum diligere quem ames,
10 nulla indigentia, nulla utilitate quaesita; quae tamen
ipsa efflorescit ex amicitia, etiam si tu eam minus
secutus sis. [101] Hac nos adulescentes benevolentia senes illos L. Paulum, M. Catonem, C. Gal-
lum, P. Nasicam, Ti. Gracchum Scipionis nostri
15 socerum, dileximus. Haec etiam magis elucet
inter aequales ut inter me et Scipionem, L. Furium,

P. Rupilium, Sp. Mummium. Vicissim autem senes in adolescentium caritate acquiescimus, ut in vestra, ut in Q. Tuberonis: equidem etiam admodum

20 adulescentis P. Rutilii, A. Verginii familiaritate delector. Quoniamque ita ratio comparata est vitae naturaeque nostrae ut alia aetas oriatur, maxime quidem optandum est ut cum aequalibus possis, quibuscum tamquam e carceribus emissus sis, cum

25 isdem ad calcem, ut dicitur, pervenire.

[102] Sed quoniam res humanae fragiles caducaeque sunt, semper aliqui anquirendi sunt quos diligamus et a quibus diligamur: caritate enim benevolentiaque sublata omnis est a vita sublata

30 iucunditas. Mihi quidem Scipio, quamquam est subito ereptus, vivit tamen semperque vivet; virtutem enim amavi illius viri quae exstincta non est. Nec mihi soli versatur ante oculos, qui illam semper in manibus habui, sed etiam posteris erit

35 clara et insignis. Nemo unquam animo aut spe maiora suscipiet qui sibi non illius memoriam atque imaginem proponendam putet.

PART 7: LINES 38–63 (THE CONCLUSION)

[103] Equidem ex omnibus rebus quas mihi aut fortuna aut natura tribuit, nihil habeo quod cum
40 amicitia Scipionis possim comparare. In hac mihi de re publica consensus, in hac rerum privatarum consilium, in eadem requies plena oblectationis fuit. Nunquam illum ne minima quidem re offendi quod quidem senserim; nihil
45 audivi ex eo ipse quod nollem. Una domus erat, idem victus isque communis; neque militia solum sed etiam peregrinationes rusticationesque communes. **[104]** Nam quid ego de studiis dicam cognoscendi semper aliquid atque discendi, in
50 quibus remoti ab oculis populi omne otiosum tempus contrivimus? Quarum rerum recordatio et memoria si una cum illo occidisset, desiderium coniunctissimi atque amantissimi viri ferre nullo modo possem. Sed nec illa exstincta sunt
55 alunturque potius et augentur cogitatione et memoria; et si illis plane orbatus essem, magnum tamen adfert mihi aetas ipsa solacium, diutius enim

iam in hoc desiderio esse non possum; omnia autem brevia tolerabilia esse debent, etiam si magna sunt.

60 Haec habui de amicitia quae dicerem. Vos autem hortor ut ita virtutem locetis, sine qua amicitia esse non potest, ut ea excepta nihil amicitia praestabilius putetis.

Literal Translations

*P*lease note that this translation tries to preserve the structure of the Latin as an aid to understanding the text. In some cases this may cause awkwardness in English. We have added words that are understood in parentheses. We have also used parentheses to provide words or phrases closer to the English construction.

SELECTION A: LINES 1–107 [SECTIONS V.17–VI.23]

[17] I can only urge you that you put friendship before all human matters; for there is nothing so fitting to nature, so suited to matters either favorable or adverse.

[18] But first I understand this thing (principle), that friendship is not able to exist except in (among) good men; nor am I pruning that thing (the definition) back to the quick as those who discuss these matters more precisely, perhaps (they discuss) correctly, but not sufficiently in relation to everyday interest; for they deny that anyone is a good man unless (he is) wise. Let it be granted so certainly; but they are calling that wisdom, which still no one mortal has attained. However, we ought to look at those things that are in use and everyday life, not those things that are imagined or desired. I would never say that Gaius Fabricius, Manius Curius, Tiberius Coruncanius, whom our ancestors judged wise, had been wise to their measure. Therefore, let them keep for themselves the name of wisdom both unacceptable and incomprehensible; let them grant that these were good men. They will not do even that; they will say that that (name) cannot be granted except to a wise man.

[19] Let us continue on, therefore, with our own dull wit, as they say. (Those) who so conduct themselves, so live that their honesty, integrity, fairness, generosity is proven, nor that there is in them any greed, lust, recklessness and that they are men of great strength of character, as those men were whom I named just now, let us consider that these (men) ought to be called good men, as they are considered, because they follow, as much as men can, nature as the best guide of (for) living well.

For it seems clear to me as follows, that we are so born that among all there is a certain connection, greater, however, as each one approaches most closely (to us). For this reason citizens have a higher priority than foreigners, relatives (a higher priority) than strangers: for nature herself has created friendship with these (people), but that (friendship) does not have enough (a great deal of) stability. For friendship is superior to family relationships in this respect, because good will can be taken away from family relationships, from friendship it cannot. For after good will has been taken away, the name of friendship is destroyed, (the name) of family relationship remains.

[20] How great the force of friendship is, moreover, can from this (the following account) be especially understood: that from the infinite connection of the human race which nature itself has brought about, (friendship) is so narrowed and reduced in measure, that every feeling of affection is joined (exists) between two people or among a few.

For friendship is nothing else if not the harmony of all divine and human matters, together with good will and affection; with wisdom excepted, I do not know in fact whether anything better than this (friendship) has been given to man by the immortal gods. Some place riches first, some good health, some power, others honors, many even (place) pleasures (first). Indeed this last (the last of these desires) is (characteristic) of brute beasts; those fleeting and uncertain desires (which I mentioned) above, however, depend not so on our plans as on the whim of fortune. (Those), however, who place the highest good in virtue, indeed they (do) very well, but this virtue itself both gives birth to friendship and sustains it; nor without virtue can friendship exist in any way.

[21] Now let us understand virtue from the habit of our life and of our conversation; and let us not measure it, as certain learned men do, by the magnificence of words; let us count those men good who are considered (good)—(men like) Paulus, the Catos, Gallus, the Scipios, Philus: ordinary life is satisfied with these (men): however, let us dismiss those who are never found at all. Therefore among such men, friendship offers such great opportunities as I can scarcely describe.

[22] First of all, how can life be "worth living" as Ennius said, which does not rest in the mutual goodwill of a friend? What is sweeter than to have (someone) with whom you may dare to speak everything just as with yourself? How would there be such great enjoyment in good times unless you were to have (someone) who might rejoice equally in them (your good times) as you yourself (do)? It would be truly difficult to bear adversity without that one who would bear those (troubles) even more seriously than you. Finally, the rest (of the enjoyments) which are sought are individually suited for the most part to individual matters; riches that you may enjoy (them); power that you may be esteemed; honors that you may be praised; pleasures that you may feel good; good health that you may lack pain and enjoy the gifts of the body: friendship embraces the greatest number (the most things). Wherever you will have turned yourself, it is at hand: it is excluded from no place: it (is) never out of season, it is never troublesome. And so we do not use water and fire, as they say (proverbially), in more places than friendship. Nor am I speaking now about commonly known or ordinary friendship, which itself, however, both delights and benefits, but about true and perfect (friendship) such as was (the friendship) of those few who are mentioned. For friendship makes favorable times more enjoyable and, dividing and sharing, (friendship makes) adverse (times) more tolerable.

[23] And since friendship embraces the most and the greatest advantages, then it certainly stands before everything because it shines forth good hope into (for) the future, nor does it allow spirits to be weakened or to fall. But in fact (one) who looks upon a friend looks upon a certain image of himself, as it were. Therefore even absent (friends) are present, and (those) needy live in abundance, and the weak are strong; and what (which) is more difficult to say, the dead live. Such regard, such great memory, such longing on the part of friends follows (after) them on account of which their death seems happy, the life of those (left behind) praiseworthy. But if you will have taken away the bond of goodwill from the nature of things, neither any home nor (any) city will be able to stand; not even the cultivation of fields will remain. If that (statement) is not understood, how great the force of friendship and harmony is can be understood from disagreements and conflicts. For what home (is) so stable, what state is so firm that cannot be entirely overturned by hatred and alienation? From which (this), how much good there is in friendship can be judged.

Selection B: Lines 1–63 [Sections XXVII.100b–104]

[100] Virtue, I say, Gaius Fannius, and you, Quintus Mucius, virtue both makes and preserves friendship. For in it (virtue) is found agreement in things (harmony of matters), in it (virtue) stability, in it (virtue) permanence which (virtue), when it has raised itself up and shown its light and has looked at and recognized the same (light) in another, it moves itself to that (light) and in turn it receives that (light) which is in another, from which, whether it be love or friendship, it bursts into flames. For each one (love and friendship) is said to come from (is named from) the word for loving; to love, however, is nothing other than to like that very person whom you love with no neediness, no advantage sought. And yet this (advantage) blossoms forth from friendship, even if you do not exactly pursue it.

[101] With this sort of good will, we as young men esteemed those old men, Lucius Paulus, Marcus Cato, Gaius Gallus, Publius Nasica, Tiberius Gracchus, the father-in-law of our Scipio. This (goodwill) shines forth even more among people of the same age, as between me and Scipio, Lucius Furius, Publius Rupilius, Spurius Mummius. In turn, moreover, as old men we find pleasure in the affection of young men, as I (do) in yours, as (I do in the affection) of Quintus Tubero: indeed I am even delighted by my close friendship of (with) the quite young Publius Rutilius and Aulus Verginius. And since the system of (our) life and of our nature has been arranged in such a way that another generation springs up, it must indeed be especially desired that you can arrive, as it were, at the goal line with (your) contemporaries, with whom you were let loose from the starting gates.

[102] But since human affairs are fragile and ephemeral, we must always seek some men whom we love and by whom we are loved: for when love and kind feelings have been taken away, all the pleasure is taken away from life. Indeed, although Scipio was suddenly taken away from me, he lives nevertheless and he will live; for I have loved the virtue of that man, which is not dead. Nor for me alone it lives before my eyes, I who had it (virtue) within reach but even for posterity it will be famous and exceptional. For no one will ever undertake greater things with courage and with hope who does not think that Scipio's memory and image should be set up (as a model).

[103] Indeed out of all those things which either fortune or nature has given to me, I have nothing which I can compare with the friendship of Scipio. In this (friendship) I had agreement about the republic (public affairs); in this (friendship) I had advice of (in) private matters; in this same (friendship), I had leisure time full of happiness. Never did I offend him in the least matter so far as I knew; I myself heard nothing from him that I did not wish. There was one home, the same way of life, and that (was) shared; not only military duty but also foreign travels and country living were shared.

[104] For what should I say about our eagerness of (for) always learning and examining something, in which, removed from the eyes of people, we spent all our leisure time? If the remembrance and the recollection of these things had died together with him, I could not bear in any manner the longing for that most closely associated and loving man. But those (remembrances) have not been lost and they are rather nourished and increased by thought and memory; and if I were entirely deprived of those, my old age itself, nevertheless, brings a great comfort; for now I cannot exist too long in this grief; all things, moreover, (which are) brief ought to be able to be endured, even if they are weighty. I had these things, at least as much as I might say, about friendship. I urge you, moreover, that you so place virtue (without which friendship is not able to exist) that, with that (virtue) excepted, you consider nothing more preferable than friendship.

Points to Ponder with Answers

The following suggestions offer a starting point to answering the Points to Ponder and are not meant to be inclusive or absolute. Close reading of the text with students should provide additional ways in which to answer these questions.

Selection A: Lines 1–107 [Sections V.17–VI.23]

Part 1: Lines 1–28

In the Stoic position, only the sapiens or philosopher/wise man is "good." Laelius' opinion is that men who have generally been accepted as "good" should be considered so. Is Laelius' opinion valid?

Stoics used the term "good" in its highest form so that good meant perfect. The term then became a measure of an ideal that could never be lived out in real life, but it set a standard. Laelius represents the practical Roman point of view. He feels that certain Roman men have set a standard for living that can serve as models for others to follow. While these men do not meet the Stoics' definition of "good," they are good role models for others.

Part 2: Lines 29–43

How does Laelius prove his argument that friendship is stronger than other natural bonds?

Laelius states that ties such as citizenship, kinship, and friendship unite people. Friendship, however, depends on affection for its existence, for if one takes all affection out of friendship, no relationship remains, but if one takes affection out of kinship, the name of kin still exists. Therefore, friendship creates a different and stronger bond than a tie produced by proximity only.

Among the hierarchy of relationships where is the bond of affection strongest?

Laelius suggests that among the hierarchy of relationships the strongest and most genuine feelings can only exist between the smallest numbers of people. Hence, the connection between two or three individuals is the most powerful. In fact, the relationship between a pair of individuals, such as Scipio and Laelius, is the ideal.

PART 3: LINES 44–65

What is the *"consensio"* in line 46 that brings people into the bond of friendship?

Consensio, as Cicero uses it here, is the agreement on all matters human and divine, accompanied by good-will and affection.

What are the priorities valued by some people that Laelius says depend on the fickle behavior of fortune?

According to Laelius, people value riches, good health, power, and public office. Pleasure is a different matter, since it is suitable only for animals and does not depend on good fortune to achieve.

According to Laelius, how does one interpret *virtus*?

Once again Laelius is making the case that his definition of "good" is the practical one, based on examples he will provide of men who fit that definition, not on the finely honed arguments of Greek philosophers.

PART 4: LINES 66–87

What specifically are the benefits of friendship mentioned by Laelius?

Friends are able to share and discuss all situations. If things go well, a friend rejoices; but if things are unfavorable, a friend feels the gravity of the situation even more seriously. Without someone to share all of life's moments, one would not have a life worth living.

Define the following words and give their benefits according to the text: *divitiae, opes, honores, voluptates, valetudo.*

divitiae: riches, for personal use
opes: power, that a person can be respected
honores: political offices, that a person can be praised
voluptates: pleasures, that a person can indulge himself
valetudo: good health, that a person can exert his body to the fullest and be without pain

Explain what Laelius means when he says: *non aqua, non igni . . . locis pluribus utimur quam amicitia.*

"Fire and water" was a formulaic expression that the Romans used to express the basic needs of life. When Laelius says "we do not use water and fire in more places than we do friendship," he states his opinion that friendship is just as much a basic need for human beings as such biological needs as water, food, and warmth.

Part 5: Lines 88–107

In line 93 (*Quocirca*) through line 96 (*vivunt*), Cicero uses a series of four opposing ideas that have to do with the simultaneous absence and presence of something. List each opposing idea and explain.

"Absent, (friends) are present": When friends are away either because of distance or death, they are still present in the hearts and minds of their friends left behind.

"Those needy live in abundance": If you have true friendship, a lack of material things is not real neediness.

"The weak are strong": If you have true friendship, the weak are no longer weak.

"The dead live": As long as the friend remains alive, the memory and love of the departed friend lives.

Describe the results of removing the *benevolentiae coniunctionem ex rerum natura*.

According to Laelius, the framework of good feelings holds every kind of society together. Without this shared good will, households, cities, and states could not thrive. With hatred and discord ubiquitous, mankind could not even manage to exist. It is this *benevolentiae coniunctionem* that holds our world together.

Explain the concept of a friend as a "second self."

Since a friend shares all the good and bad times of one's life, that friend becomes an *exemplar* (image) of one's self. When friends see and talk to one another, it is as if they speak or interact with themselves. There is never a fear of rejection but rather a sharing and dividing of joys and sorrows. This is why friendship is such a powerful force for individuals.

Selection B: Lines 1–63 [Sections XXVII.100b–104]

Part 6: Section 100, Lines 1–37

In lines 89–91 [VII.23] of the Selection A (*amicitia . . . praelucet*); and in the Selection B, first in line 4 [XXVII.100] (*[virtus] . . . ostendit lumen*) and then in line 15 [XXVII. 101] (*[benevolentia] . . . elucet*), Cicero makes use of light imagery. Examine each of these uses and explain the effect of this figurative language.

In these passages of the text Cicero describes *amicitia* (friendship), *virtus* (virtue) and *benevolentia* (affection for one's fellow man) as forces of light (*lumen*), blazing forth (*exardescit*) and providing a beacon of hope for the future (*praelucet*). Since Cicero has been sparing in his use of figurative language, this imagery vividly makes the point to the reader that *amicitia, virtus* and *benevolentia* are intimately connected as powerful forces for good for mankind. The imagery thus reinforces Cicero's major theme about the supreme importance to human beings of virtue, friendship, and good will toward others.

As a man ages, he has friendships with elders, contemporaries, and finally with those younger than himself. Explain the advantages of each of these situations.

When one is an adolescent student, such as Scipio and Laelius were in their youth, one is guided and molded through associations with older teachers and philosophers. These older men guided through their wisdom. It is with contemporaries that one feels most comfortable, and Laelius wishes that they could all pass through the various phases of their lives together, including aging and death. Finally as an older man, it is Laelius' turn to guide younger men such as his sons-in-law, as he does throughout the *De Amicitia*.

In what way will Scipio serve as an example in the present and in the future?

For Laelius, Scipio (even though recently dead) lives and always will live for his *virtus*. *Virtus* (virtue) has not perished and Laelius remembers the right actions of his friend. Since Scipio was a well-known person in Rome, he will also be remembered. Therefore, Scipio's example of a life lived according to principle will serve as an example to future generations.

PART 7: LINES 38–63 (CONCLUSION)

Describe in detail the life that Scipio and Laelius shared.

No two friends could serve as better examples of a friend as a second self than Laelius and Scipio. They had a complete agreement about the Republic, private matters, and the enjoyment of leisure time. They never offended one another in speech. They shared the same way of life. They traveled together on military campaigns and other foreign excursions, including time spent at their country estates. They studied together and read the same books in their leisure.

How is Laelius able to bear Scipio's loss?

Laelius says that he would not be able to bear Scipio's loss if it were not for the memory of the life he and Scipio spent together. His recollections are nourished and increased in his thoughts. If it were not for his memory of shared times, Laelius states that he would be glad to die.

Based on your reading of the essay as a whole, how has Laelius demonstrated that there is nothing more valuable than friendship and that it cannot be obtained without moral worth or goodness (*virtus*)?

Laelius spent much time explaining that only good men can have good friendships because friendship depends on right actions and the desire that one's friend should be treated even better than oneself. Moral rightness is necessary for the bonds of society, and especially friendship, to exist. Laelius demonstrated that goals such as riches, good health, and public honors are more dependent on the whim of fortune whereas friendship contains all the good qualities that make life worth living: stability, constancy, love. No one is alone who has a true friend, one with whom everything is shared and divided. Without this friendship, life would not be worth living. Finally, friendship endures even after the life of one's friend has passed, since the memories live on and comfort one.

Sample Assessments

*W*e have written the following assessments in accordance with the Advanced Placement testing mode: a translation passage, a spot question, and a brief essay. In addition, there are questions on vocabulary meanings in context and grammar if the teacher wishes to use these.

ASSESSMENT I: [17–20]

I. Spot Question

1   Agamus igitur pingui Minerva, ut aiunt. Qui ita se gerunt, ita vivunt, ut eorum
2   probetur fides, integritas, aequitas, liberalitas, nec sit in eis ulla cupiditas, libido,
3   audacia, sintque magna constantia, ut ei fuerunt modo quos nominavi, hos viros
4   bonos, ut habiti sunt, sic etiam appellandos putemus, quia sequantur quantum
5   homines possunt naturam optimam bene vivendi ducem.

1. Name a figure of speech that occurs in line 1 (*Agamus . . . aiunt*) and write out the Latin that illustrates it.

2. What group of people is referred to in lines 1–2 (*Qui . . . liberalitas*)?

3. From lines 2–3 (*nec . . . audacia*) write out the Latin and translate at least two negative qualities that a person might possess.

4. In lines 4–5 (*ut . . . ducem*), how does Laelius think that certain people should be considered, and why?

II. Translate the passage below as literally as possible.

Sic enim mihi perspicere videor, ita natos esse nos ut inter omnes esset societas quaedam, maior autem, ut quisque proxime accederet. Itaque cives potiores quam peregrini, propinqui quam alieni: cum his enim amicitiam natura ipsa peperit, sed ea non satis habet firmitatis. Namque hoc praestat amicitia propinquitati quod ex propinquitate benevolentia tolli potest, ex amicitia non potest: sublata enim benevolentia amicitiae nomen tollitur, propinquitatis manet.

III. Essay

1   Divitias alii praeponunt, bonam alii valetudinem, alii potentiam, alii honores, multi
2   etiam voluptates. Beluarum hoc quidem extremum; illa autem superiora caduca et
3   incerta, posita non tam in consiliis nostris quam in fortunae temeritate. Qui autem
4   in virtute summum bonum ponunt, praeclare illi quidem, sed haec ipsa virtus
5   amicitiam et gignit et continet, nec sine virtute amicitia esse ullo pacto potest.

6   Laelius. Ego vos hortari tantum possum ut amicitiam omnibus rebus humanis
7   anteponatis; nihil est enim tam naturae aptum, tam conveniens ad res vel secundas
8   vel adversas.

In the passages above, Laelius offers several options concerning the possessions which some people value in life. Identify these possessions, tell why he rejects them, and discuss the choice and reasons for the choice that Laelius makes.

Cite the Latin words from throughout the passage that support the assertions in your essay. Translate or paraphrase the Latin words you cite. It is your responsibility to make it clear that what is written is based on your knowledge of the Latin text and not merely on a general recollection of the passage.

IV. Give the meanings for the words in bold according to context.

Sed hoc primum **sentio** nisi in bonis amicitiam esse non posse; neque id ad vivum reseco, ut illi qui haec subtilius disserunt, **fortasse** vere, sed ad communem utilitatem parum; negant enim **quemquam** virum bonum esse nisi sapientem. Sit ita sane; sed eam sapientiam interpretantur quam **adhuc** mortalis nemo est consecutus. Nos **autem** ea quae sunt in usu vitaque communi, non ea quae finguntur aut **optantur,** spectare **debemus.** Nunquam ego dicam C. Fabricium, M'. Curium, Ti. Coruncanium, quos sapientes nostri maiores iudicabant, ad istorum normam fuisse sapientes. Qua re sibi **habeant** sapientiae nomen et invidiosum et obscurum; **concedant** ut hi boni viri fuerint. **Ne** id **quidem facient** negabunt id nisi sapienti posse **concedi.**

1. sentio	7. debemus
2. fortasse	8. habeant
3. quemquam	9. concedant
4. adhuc	10. ne . . . quidem
5. autem	11. facient
6. optantur	12. concedi

V. Answer the grammar questions about the words in bold according to context.

Quanta autem vis amicitiae **sit** ex hoc **intellegi** maxime potest, quod ex infinita societate generis humani, **quam** conciliavit ipsa natura, ita contracta res est et adducta in angustum ut omnis caritas aut inter duos aut inter paucos **iungeretur.**

Est autem amicitia nihil aliud nisi omnium divinarum humanarumque rerum cum benevolentia et **caritate consensio;** qua quidem haud scio an **excepta sapientia** nil unquam melius homini sit **a dis immortalibus** datum.

1.	sit	Give the mood of the verb; translate.
2.	intellegi	Give the name of the form; translate.
3.	quam	What is the antecedent of this word?
4.	iungeretur	Give the tense of the verb and the type of subjunctive.
5.	caritate	What is the case of this word?
6.	consensio	What is the case of this word?
7.	excepta sapientia	In what construction are these words? Translate.
8.	a dis immortalibus	What grammatical term describes these words? Translate.

ASSESSMENT II: [21–23]

I. Spot Question

1   Cumque plurimas et maximas commoditates amicitia contineat, tum illa
2   nimirum praestat omnibus, quod bonam spem praelucet in posterum nec debilitari
3   animos aut cadere patitur. Verum enim amicum qui intuetur, tamquam exemplar
4   aliquod intuetur sui. Quocirca et absentes adsunt et egentes abundant et imbecilli
5   valent, et, quod difficilius dictu est, mortui vivunt; tantus eos honos, memoria,
6   desiderium prosequitur amicorum, ex quo illorum beata mors videtur, horum vita
7   laudabilis.

1. In lines 1–3 (*Cumque . . . patitur*), write out the Latin and translate two reasons that explain why friendship is important.

2. In lines 3–4 (*Verum . . . sui*), to what is looking at a friend compared?

3. In lines 4–5 (*Quocirca . . . vivunt*), write out and identify a figure of speech.

4. In lines 5–7 (*tantus . . . laudabilis*), write out the Latin and translate at least one contrast.

II. Translate the passage below as literally as possible.

Quod si exemeris ex rerum natura benevolentiae coniunctionem, nec domus ulla nec urbs stare poterit; ne agri quidem cultus permanebit. Id si minus intellegitur, quanta vis amicitiae concordiaeque sit ex dissensionibus atque discordiis percipi potest. Quae enim domus tam stabilis, quae tam firma civitas est, quae non odiis atque discidiis funditus possit everti? ex quo quantum boni sit in amicitia iudicari potest.

III. Essay

1 Principio, qui potest esse vita vitalis, ut ait Ennius, quae non in amici mutua
2 benevolentia conquiescat? Quid dulcius quam habere quicum omnia audeas sic
3 loqui ut tecum? Qui esset tantus fructus in prosperis rebus, nisi haberes qui illis
4 aeque ac tu ipse gauderet? Adversas vero ferre difficile esset sine eo qui illas
5 gravius etiam quam tu ferret. Denique ceterae res quae expetuntur opportunae
6 sunt singulae rebus fere singulis; divitiae ut utare; opes ut colare; honores ut
7 laudere; voluptates ut gaudeas; valetudo ut dolore careas et muneribus fungare
8 corporis: amicitia res plurimas continet. Quoquo te verteris praesto est: nullo
9 loco excluditur: nunquam intempestiva, nunquam molesta est. Itaque non aqua,
10 non igni, ut aiunt, locis pluribus utimur quam amicitia.

In the passage above, Laelius presents his idea of a "life worth living." In a short essay discuss the difference between what Laelius values and what others might choose and the importance of each of the choices.

Cite the Latin words from throughout the passage that support the assertions in your essay. Translate or paraphrase the Latin words you cite. It is your responsibility to make it clear that what is written is based on your knowledge of the Latin text and not merely on a general recollection of the passage.

IV. Give the meanings for the words in bold according to context.

Neque ego nunc de vulgari aut de mediocri, **quae** tamen **ipsa et** delectat et prodest, sed de vera et perfecta **loquor,** qualis eorum qui pauci nominantur **fuit.** Nam et **secundas** res splendidiores facit amicitia, et adversas partiens communicansque **leviores.**

Iam virtutem ex **consuetudine** vitae sermonisque nostri **interpretemur,** nec eam, ut quidam docti, verborum magnificentia metiamur, virosque bonos eos qui habentur numeremus, Paulos, Catones, Gallos, Scipiones, Philos: his communis vita contenta est: eos autem omittamus qui **omnino** nusquam **reperiuntur. Tales** igitur inter viros amicitia tantas opportunitates habet quantas **vix queo** dicere.

1. quae	8. consuetudine
2. ipsa	9. interpretemur
3. et	10. omnino
4. loquor	11. reperiuntur
5. fuit	12. tales
6. secundas	13. vix
7. leviores	14. queo

Assessment III: [100–104]

I. Spot Question

1   Sed quoniam res humanae fragiles caducaeque sunt, semper aliqui
2   anquirendi sunt quos diligamus et a quibus diligamur: caritate enim
3   benevolentiaque sublata omnis est a vita sublata iucunditas. Mihi quidem
4   Scipio, quamquam est subito ereptus, vivit tamen semperque vivet; virtutem
5   enim amavi illius viri quae exstincta non est. Nec mihi soli versatur ante
6   oculos, qui illam semper in manibus habui, sed etiam posteris erit clara et
7   insignis. Nemo unquam animo aut spe maiora suscipiet qui sibi non illius
8   memoriam atque imaginem proponendam putet.

1. In lines 1–2 (*Sed . . . diligamur*), what actions does Laelius offer to counteract the uncertainty of life?

2. Name a figure of speech (other than alliteration) that occurs in lines 3–4 and write out the Latin that illustrates it.

3. In line 4 (*virtutem . . . est*), explain the manner in which Scipio's influence continues.

4. In lines 5–7 (*Nec mihi . . . putet*), write out the Latin that expresses a contrast and explain the two events which are represented by that contrast.

II. Translate the passage below as literally as possible.

Quoniamque ita ratio comparata est vitae naturaeque nostrae ut alia aetas oriatur, maxime quidem optandum est ut cum aequalibus possis, quibuscum tamquam e carceribus emissus sis, cum isdem ad calcem, ut dicitur, pervenire.

III. Essay

1   Equidem ex omnibus rebus quas mihi aut fortuna aut natura tribuit, nihil habeo quod
2   cum amicitia Scipionis possim comparare. In hac mihi de re publica consensus, in hac
3   rerum privatarum consilium, in eadem requies plena oblectationis fuit. Nunquam illum
4   ne minima quidem re offendi quod quidem senserim; nihil audivi ex eo ipse quod
5   nollem. Una domus erat, idem victus isque communis; neque militia solum sed etiam
6   peregrinationes rusticationesque communes. Nam quid ego de studiis dicam
7   cognoscendi semper aliquid atque discendi, in quibus remoti ab oculis populi omne
8   otiosum tempus contrivimus? Quarum rerum recordatio et memoria si una cum illo
9   occidisset, desiderium coniunctissimi atque amantissimi viri ferre nullo modo possem.

In the passage above, Laelius illustrates the scope of his friendship with Scipio. In a short essay, discuss the full nature of their friendship and its effects on Laelius even after Scipio's death. Refer specifically to the Latin throughout the passage to support the points you make in your essay.

Cite the Latin words from throughout the passage that support the assertions in your essay. Translate or paraphrase the Latin words you cite. It is your responsibility to make it clear that what is written is based on your knowledge of the Latin text and not merely on a general recollection of the passage.

IV. Give the meanings for the words in bold according to context.

Virtus, virtus, inquam, C. Fanni et tu, Q. Muci, et conciliat amicitias et conservat. In ea est enim convenientia rerum, in ea stabilitas, in ea constantia, quae cum se extulit et **ostendit** lumen suum et idem **adspexit** agnovitque in alio, ad id se admovet **vicissim**que accipit illud quod in altero est, ex quo exardescit sive amor sive amicitia. **Utrumque** enim dictum est ab amando; amare autem nihil aliud est nisi eum ipsum diligere quem ames, nulla indigentia, nulla utilitate **quaesita;** quae tamen ipsa **efflorescit** ex amicitia, etiam si tu eam minus secutus sis.

1. ostendit
2. adspexit
3. vicissim

4. utrumque
5. quaesita
6. efflorescit

Sed nec illa exstincta sunt alunturque **potius** et **augentur** cogitatione et memoria; et si illis plane orbatus essem, magnum tamen adfert mihi **aetas** ipsa **solacium, diutius** enim iam in hoc desiderio esse non possum; omnia autem brevia tolerabilia esse debent, **etiam** si magna sunt.

1. potius
2. augentur
3. aetas

4. solacium
5. diutius
6. etiam

V. Answer the grammar questions about the words in bold according to context.

Haec habui de amicitia quae dicerem. Vos autem hortor ut ita virtutem **locetis,** sine **qua** amicitia esse non potest, ut **ea excepta** nihil **amicitia** praestabilius **putetis.**

1.	locetis	What is the tense of this verb? In what type of subjunctive clause is it?
2.	qua	What is the antecedent of this word? Translate.
3.	ea excepta	In what construction are these words? Translate.
4.	amicitia	What is the case and use of this word?
5.	putetis	What is the tense of this word? In what type of subjunctive clause is it?

Discussion Questions

Before beginning the readings from *Cicero: De Amicitia Selections*, students should be encouraged to do some thinking about the subject of friendship. A brief writing assignment and exploration of the following topics should stimulate their interest in Cicero's subject.

1. Define friendship.

2. How do you select friends?

3. Describe an ideal friend.

4. What sort of things would you share with a friend?

5. What differences are there between "best friends" and acquaintances?

Students should become familiar with the setting of the work. Some time should be spent discussing Laelius and Scipio in their historical context. A class discussion of these characters, and Cicero's purpose in using the setting of Laelius' garden for the discussion of the topic with his sons-in-law, will lay the background for the work.

SECTIONS 17–19 (LINES 1–28)

Have students discuss the contrast between the philosophers' definition of a "good" man and Laelius' more practical discussion of men in Roman history whom he and others call "good." Lead students into thinking about the importance of defining terms such as a "good" man and the concept of using historical people as examples for the living.

SECTIONS 19–20 (LINES 29–43)

Discuss the concept that people are brought together by common bonds and that the greater the proximity the closer the bond. Make sure that students understand that friendship is the closest bond and that it can only exist between two or only a very few. Ask them to give examples of these concepts from their own experiences.

SECTIONS 20–22 (LINES 44–87)

In these sections, Laelius talks about what some people think are important possessions and attainments in life. Laelius concludes this list by stating his own view that virtue is the highest goal because it gives birth to and sustains friendship. As a way of introducing this section, instruct the students to make a list of the five things that are most important to them. These can be discussed in class. When the students read Laelius' list, they can determine if they would like to amend their own lists.

Section 23 (lines 88–107)

Students should talk about the concept of a friend as a second self and why friendship ties society together.

Sections 100–101 (lines 1 – 25)

Students should talk about Laelius' attention to terms. He talks about *amor* and *amicitia* and *diligere* and *amare*. His focus is that when a person has love for another (*amor*), then the lover also likes that person and cares about his well being (*diligere*).

Students should also discuss the relationships that exist throughout life such as the ones Laelius recounts. During youth, he found guidance from older men whom he admired; as a mature man, he took comfort from his peers; and now, as an old man, he enjoys the affection of younger men, such as his sons-in-law.

Sections 102–103 (lines 26–63)

It is important for students to understand the closeness of the relationship between Scipio and Laelius. Students might be asked to relate the shared experiences of Laelius and Scipio and discuss why it is that Laelius is able to bear his grief.

Finally students should discuss what the friendship between Laelius and Scipio has taught them about friendship both in general and personally.

Annotated Bibliography

BOOKS

Epstein, J. *Friendship: An Exposé.* Boston: Houghton Miffin, 2006. A modern examination of friendship. Witty and provocative. Chapter 6 provides a quick history of past studies, including the ancients.

Everitt, A. Cicero. *The Life and Times of Rome's Greatest Politician.* New York: Random House, 2001. Recent bestseller, available in paperback. Has received mixed reviews from scholars but it does provide a readable introduction to Cicero's life and the period. Relies on ancient sources but weak on modern scholarship.

Gotoff, Harry. *Cicero's Elegant Style: An Analysis of the Pro Archia.* Urbana: University of Illinois Press, 1979. This study provides a sentence by sentence analysis of Cicero's rhetoric and his Latin artistry. Students will find this book difficult but teachers should appreciate that the light it sheds on the *Pro Archia* will be useful for appreciating the *De Amicitia.* Currently out of print.

Konstan, D. *Friendship in the Classical World.* Cambridge: Cambridge University Press, 1997. Thorough introduction to ancient views on friendship in Greece and Rome; similarities and differences with modern views are also examined. Useful for providing a context for Cicero's views.

Morford, M. *Roman Philosophers.* New York: Routledge, 2002. Contains an excellent chapter on Cicero as the most influential of Roman philosophers. A short discussion of the *De Amicitia* places this dialogue in the context of ancient philosophical discussion.

Powell, J. G. F., ed. *Cicero the Philosopher: Twelve Papers.* Oxford: Clarendon Press, 1999. While not directly concerned with the *De Amicitia,* the introduction gives a very good overview of the historical and intellectual context of Cicero's philosophical works.

Rawson, E. *Cicero: A Portrait.* Ithaca, NY: Cornell University Press, 1983. Must reading for students, this biography has received strong reviews and stood the test of time.

Scullard, H. H. *From the Gracchi to Nero: A History of Rome from 133 BC to AD 68.* Fifth edition. New York: Routledge, 1982. Still a good introduction to this momentous period in Roman history.

Wood, N. *Cicero's Social and Political Thought.* Berkeley: University of California Press, 1988. A careful study of Cicero as social and political thinker. Students may find the discussion of political theory difficult. Especially recommended are the chapters on Ciceronian society and Cicero's life and works.

ARTICLES

Brunt, P. A. "'Amicitia' in the Late Roman Republic." In Robin Seager, ed., *The Crisis of the Roman Republic*. Cambridge: Heffer, 1969, 199–218. A now-classic discussion of the various kinds of relationships, political and private, covered by the term, *amicitia*.

Habinek, T. N. "Toward a History of Friendly Advice: The Politics of Candor in Cicero's *De Amicitia*." *Aperion* 23 (1990) 165–85. I have not seen this article.

Leach, E. W. "Absence and Desire in Cicero's *De Amicitia*." *CW* 87 (1993) 3–20. A careful reading of the dialogue, focusing on "the way in which the historical perspective of the dialogue enforces this crisis of separation (from the recently deceased Scipio) and its implications for the structure and consistency of Cicero's argument."

Powell, J. G. F. "The Manuscripts and Text of Cicero's *Laelius de Amicitia*." *CQ* 48.2 (1988) 506–518. A definitive study of the textual tradition for the *De Amicitia*.

Singh, K. L. "On Friendship." In P. MacKendrick, *The Philosophical Books of Cicero*, 213–222. New York: St. Martin's Press, 1989. A very close discussion of the *De Amicitia* from a rhetorical and philosophical point of view.

Williams, M. F. "Catullus 50 and the Language of Friendship." *Latomus* 47 (1988) 69–73. Makes a connection between the language of Catullus 50 and *De Amicitia* XXVII, 100, regarding the beginning of friendship as "blazing forth."

COMMENTARIES

Gould, H. E., and J. L. Whiteley. *Cicero de Amicitia*. Macmillan & Co., 1941. Reprint, Wauconda, IL: Bolchazy-Carducci, 2004. Provides a bare bones introduction and commentary to the dialogue.

Powell, J. G. F. *Cicero: On Friendship and the Dream of Scipio*. Warminster: Aris and Phillips, 1990. Excellent introduction to the philosophical underpinnings of the *De Amicitia*. Also contains the best Latin text available, a translation, and commentary.

ADDITIONAL ASSISTANCE

Ancient History Sourcebook: Cicero: Translation of *On Friendship* or *Laelius* at http://www.fordham.edu/halsall/ancient/cicero-friendship.html

In the near future CW will be publishing an issue devoted to the teaching of *De Amicitia*, edited by Judith de Luce. For an innovative approach to teaching this text see de Luce's "Teaching Cicero's Laelius de Amicitia" http://montgomery.cas.muohio.edu/delucej/cls322/deamdeluce.html. Of special interest is the bibliography of scholarship from other disciplines, such as sociology and gerontology.

CICERO ANCILLARY MATERIALS

CICERO: Pro Archia Poeta Oratio, 2nd Ed.
Student Text by Steven M. Cerutti; Teacher's Guide by Linda A. Fabrizio

Cicero's Pro Archia Poeta Oratio is one of the best defenses of literature and the humanities. Cerutti's edition provides a comprehensive treatment of grammatical issues with a keen analysis of the rhetorical devices Cicero wove into the fabric of the oration.

This edition combines the Latin text, running vocabulary and commentary, a brief bibliography, glossary of proper names and places, glossary of terms, and general vocabulary to make it an excellent edition for the AP* and college Latin classroom.

The new *Pro Archia Poeta Oratio* Teacher's Guide by Linda A. Fabrizio is designed to meet the needs of the busy AP* teacher. It includes the oration in large print suitable for photocopying, a literal translation of the oration, a select bibliography, and a set of assessments/questions with sample answers.

Student Text: xxviii + 132 pp (2006) Paperback 6" x 9" ISBN 978-0-86516-642-4
Teacher's Guide: (2006) Paperback 8.5" x 11" ISBN 978-0-86516-616-5

A Must for Every Teacher. A Desideratum for Each Student.

CICERO PRO ARCHIA POETA ORATIO
A Structural Analysis of the Speech
and Companion to the Commentary
Steven Cerutti

The "COMPANION" was written to accompany *Cicero: Pro Archia Poeta Oratio*, but makes an excellent independent resource for all *Pro Archia* texts.

Comprehensive diagrams and detailed sentence-by-sentence analysis provide the student with a reliable road map through the periodic structure of the Ciceronian sentence.

Features:
- Introduction, "Reading the Diagrams"
- Latin text with same-page and facing
  - Translation
  - Notes & Discussion
  - Latin text in sentence diagrams

xii + 118 pp (1999) Paperback 6" x 9" ISBN 978-0-86516-439-0

This "WORKING" in Cicero is a Must for Students to Excel!

A CICERO WORKBOOK
Jane Webb Crawford and Judith Hayes

This workbook, part of the "Latin Workbook Series," contains the Latin text that is on the AP* syllabus accompanied by exercises (grammar, translation, short answer analysis, figures of speech, and essay questions) that will both help students to read and understand the literature as well as to prepare for the AP* examination. The Teacher's Manual features the entire student text along with the answers.

Student Text: (2006) Paperback 8.5" x 11" ISBN 978-0-86516-643-1
Teacher's Manual: (Forthcoming) Paperback 6" x 9" ISBN 978-0-86516-654-7

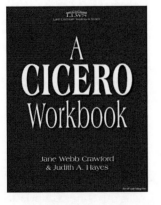

*AP is a registered trademark of the College Entrance Examination Board, which was not involved in the production of, and does not endorse, this product.

BOLCHAZY-CARDUCCI PUBLISHERS, INC.
WWW.BOLCHAZY.COM

CICERO ANCILLARY MATERIALS

Dramatic Reading of the Entire Pro Archia in Restored Classical Pronunciation.

THE LIVING VOICE OF LATIN: Cicero: Selections
Read by Robert P. Sonkowsky

Cicero Selections: *In Catilinam* I (complete), *Pro Archia* (complete), selections from other speeches of Cicero, from his rhetorical and philosophical treatises, and from his poetry.

Booklet and 2 cassettes, Order #23680

O tempora, o mores: A Brief Vita of Cicero.

CICERO THE PATRIOT
Rose Williams

Light-hearted in tone but faithful to the facts, this volume interweaves Cicero's private life and feelings with the development of his public life and literary output. Supplementary materials make this an invaluable resource for both students and teachers.

Features: • Complete description of events and historical circumstances of Cicero's life • Timeline of events and publication of Cicero's works • Glossary of terms • One-page summary of Cicero's life

Teacher's Manual Features: • Suggestions for study enrichment • Sample report topics • Further information for the teacher • Thought questions for students • Quick questions to test comprehension

Student Text: vi + 92 pp. (2004) Paperback 6" x 9" ISBN 978-0-86516-587-8
Teacher's Manual: xi + 74 pp. (2004) Paperback 6" x 9" ISBN 978-0-86516-588-5

PERFORMING CICERO'S SPEECHES
An Experimental Workshop
a video by Jon Hall and Robin Bond

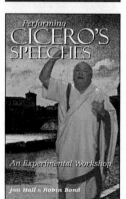

How exactly did Cicero perform his speeches? This video uses guidelines on voice and gesture from rhetorical treatises to reconstruct Cicero's oratorical delivery in a theatrical workshop environment.

Features: • Passages discussed and performed from six of Cicero's speeches: *Pro Caelio, Pro Milone, Pro Ligario, Pro Archia, In Catilinam 2, Philippics 6* • Booklet with complete Latin texts and translations • Bibliography • Restored Classical Pronunciation! But much more!

VHS Videotape (32 minutes) and Booklet (2003) ISBN 978-0-86516-488-8

Cicero—he stood alone against Rome's tyrants!

THE LOCK
Benita Kane Jaro

The Lock, though it is a completely independent novel, continues the portrait of the collapsing Roman society of the late Republic so brilliantly depicted in *The Key.* The principal figures of the age—poets, scholars, soldiers, politicians, powerful political women, even slaves, Julius Caesar, Cicero, Pompey the Great—all make their appearance and play out their fateful struggle.

Benita Kane Jaro is an exciting writer of great skill and grace. Courage, too...The result is a powerful and moving story, as freshly minted as today's news and as haunting as the deepest memory.

–George Garrett

If there is to be a worthy successor to Mary Renault, or to Marguerite Yourcenar, it may be Benita Kane Jaro.
–Doris Grumbach

xxii + 282 pp, original illustrations (2002) Paperback ISBN 978-0-86516-535-9

BOLCHAZY-CARDUCCI PUBLISHERS, INC.
WWW.BOLCHAZY.COM